D1243651

Zola: Photographer

Zola
Photographer

François Émile-Zola
and Massin

Translated from the French by
Liliane Emery Tuck

SEAVER BOOKS
Henry Holt and Company
New York

Published in the United States by Seaver Books/Henry Holt and Company
115 West 18th Street, New York, New York 10011.
Published in Canada by Fitzhenry & Whiteside Limited,
195 Allstate Parkway, Markham, Ontario L3R 4T8.
Original edition published in France under the title
Zola photographe, copyright © 1979 Editions Denoël.

Library of Congress Cataloging-in-Publication Data
Zola, Émile, 1840–1902.
[Zola photographe. English]
Zola—photographer / [compiled and edited by] François Émile-Zola
and Massin; translated from the French by Liliane Emery Tuck.—
1st American ed.
p. cm.
Revised translation of: Zola photographe.
Bibliography: p.
1. Photography. Artistic. 2. Zola, Émile, 1840–1902. 3. France–
–Social life and customs—Pictorial works.   I. Émile-Zola,
François, 1917–   II. Massin.   III. Title.
TR652.Z6413   1988
770′.92′4—dc19
[B]   88-6742
                                                                      CIP

ISBN 0-8050-0747-4

First American Edition

Designer: Massin

Printed in the United States of America
1   3   5   7   9   10   8   6   4   2

Contents

Acknowledgments

Most of the documents reproduced in this work come from the collection of Émile Zola's grandson Dr. François Émile-Zola. Other photographs were provided to us by another grandson of Émile Zola, M. Jean-Claude Le Blond, to whom we express our thanks for the help he was willing to give us.

Our gratitude extends equally to Mme Morin-Laborde, who shared with us documents hitherto unknown; to Mme Colette Becker, who gave us her advice and allowed us to benefit from her work on Zola; to Professor Jean-Claude Cassaing from the University of Limoges; and to M. Rodolphe Walter, who gave us access to copies made from the original photographs.

We also wish to thank Éditions Fasquelle, MM. Henri Mitterand, and Lewis Thorpe (the English editor of *Pages d'exil*), who gave us permission to reprint extracts from the books and articles they published; Éditions Gallimard, which provided us with the *Album Zola* documents; M. François Lemans, archivist, and the Kodak-Pathé Company.

Other Zola material emanates from the Zola Museum in Médan and the Zola centers in Toronto and Paris.

Zola: Photographer

1

At the end of the last century, in 1888, photography grew even more popular when George Eastman introduced the first of his cameras, the Box model. Émile Zola, too, became an enthusiast of this art, which had established itself over the past several decades.

How did Zola become interested in photography? We may guess that he wanted to amass material for future novels: the photographic lens allowed him to prolong direct observation and played the role of a notebook. But in 1888, the major part of *Les Rougon-Macquart* was already written, and if the pages of the present work reveal the novelist's interest in trains and locomotives, the reader may be disappointed to learn that these snapshots of the Paris–Le Havre train at full speed were taken at least five years after *La Bête humaine*. For the truth is Zola did not really begin to practice photography until 1894. During the eight years that followed (until his death in 1902), he would take several thousand photographs.

In August of 1888, Zola was at Royan with Georges Charpentier, his editor; the engraver Fernand Desmoulin; and the Labordes, cousins of his wife, Alexandrine. In addition, Alexandrine had brought along her seamstress, a young woman named Jeanne Rozerot. Zola appeared to be in high spirits and taking full advantage of his holidays. He was photographed in an alpine costume with his friends; he took boat rides with them. And it was during that summer as well that Victor Billaud, the writer, poet, editor,

2

1. Zola photographing in the Bois de Boulogne. 2. Holidays in Royan: Zola is in the middle, his back to the mast.

3

3. Félix Tournachon, known as Nadar, was born in 1820 and lived to be ninety. His illustrious career included photography, caricature, journalism, and aeronautics. (Photographic Archives. © SPADEM) 4. Holidays in Royan: during a meal outdoors, Zola (in the back and to the right) lifts his glass. 5. Three vacationers in casual but elegant attire. From left to right: the editor Georges Charpentier, Zola, the engraver Fernand Desmoulin. Zola had two revelations in 1888: the love of Jeanne Rozerot and the love of photography (thanks to Victor Billaud). 6. Zola and his Box camera.

and journalist of Royan who had joined the group, introduced the writer to photography. However, the influence of eminent professionals was no doubt more determining: Zola counted Étienne Carjat, Pierre Petit, and Nadar among his friends.

The writer's first meeting with Nadar dates back to the 1860s. The setting was the Café Guerbois, near the place Clichy, a meeting place for such painters as Manet (to whom Zola introduced Cézanne), as well as those who would be refused at the Salon of 1866. Nadar, a member of the Société des Gens de Lettres, of which Zola became president in 1891, did a series of portraits of the author between 1876 and 1898. From the correspondence that ensued, only twenty or so letters have been recovered, but we can surmise that the writer asked Nadar to introduce him to certain secrets of his art. A journalist, Nadar in 1854 had published *Panthéon des gloires contemporaines*, in which the pictures were often traced from photographic portraits. And, in 1876, "to redo the *Panthéon* from memory," it was to Zola that Nadar first addressed himself.

Thus, at the end of the century and among his peers, Zola was the writer most passionate about photography. He bought no fewer than ten cameras—enough to satisfy the most exacting professional—several of which were equipped with features that would surprise us today. He installed three darkrooms in the basements of his various homes; he perfected a shutter release system that allowed

4

5

4

"Please forgive me for having kept you waiting. It's the time of day I usually devote to my new hobby, photography. When you arrived, I was in the middle of developing a few snapshots I took this afternoon at the World's Fair. Every man should have a hobby and I confess to my extreme passion for mine. In my opinion, you cannot say that you have seen something in its entirety unless you have taken a picture of it, which reveals all sorts of details which otherwise would not be discerned. Now, take a seat and tell me what I can do for you."
(Extract from an interview Zola gave to the English magazine The King *in 1900)*

8

7. The photographer photographed (by Jeanne). 8. Jeanne Rozerot and the two children Zola had by her, Denise and Jacques. Jeanne holds the case of the Jumelle Carpentier in her lap.

9
10

On April 15, 1898, tired from the numerous sessions of his trial, Émile Zola is resting in his country home in Médan. In an interview he tells Philippe Dubois, a reporter for L'Aurore: "I was in my lab, developing. I have taken a lot of photographs lately—landscapes as well as people. I find it all extremely interesting."

At the end of July 1899, a month and a half after his self-imposed exile, Zola was interviewed again by the same journalist: "If you'll pardon my indiscretion, sir, could you elaborate on the pictures you were developing?"

"Zola: 'There are shots of England, hotels, London pubs, as well as crippled bums in rags. I shot 300 pictures with a small, 2.9 × 3.9 (cm) camera that I hooked on the handlebar of my bicycle when I went for a ride. With it, I was able to take terrifically clear pictures. I shall gather these pictures together in an album that I'll call: the album of Exile. It will contain interesting documents and various memorabilia. Unfortunately, during the trip, 4 developed negatives got broken. One of those represented an admirable window display of a flower shop where each morning I used to buy a fresh bouquet for my wife when she was ill.'

"And, with the nostalgia shared by all amateur photographers, Zola added: 'Naturally, the lost negatives were the best ones.' Zola went back to his lab as soon as I left."

11

12

9 to 11. Zola photographs Jeanne Dutard, the daughter of his editor, Georges Charpentier.   12. The man standing to Jeanne Dutard's left is her husband, Henry.

13

14

"My dear Linette, At last, I received your letter this morning! . . . Yesterday, your uncle wanted to develop 24 negatives, it's been pouring torrents of rain since this morning and despite his wish that I should help him, which I would have been glad to do in fine dry weather, I let him lock himself up in that damp little laboratory while warning him at the same time that it wasn't very hygienic especially after lunch. Nonetheless, he was obstinate and, for two and a half hours, he remained in the dark, raving and mumbling nonsense to himself because he hadn't put in the plates right. In short, the result was that he became very ill after his prolonged stay in the laboratory." (Alexandrine Zola to her young cousin Élina Laborde, August 9, 1897)

"You are very kind, my dear Georges, to thank me for the prints which your mother brought you. They are mediocre and I would not have offered them to you, wishing to give you better ones, which I shall do. Here, I have only very old paper, and my new darkroom, with which I am not familiar, plays inexplicable tricks on me. The enlarger that I have in Paris is much more reliable and if you want me to enlarge the prints for you it would be best to await my return.

"Photography is in fact full of mysteries and disappointments and it would be wrong of you to complain about a few failures at the beginning. As with all things, one must persevere, take all things into consideration and then, proceed with the utmost patience and the utmost logic possible." (Zola to Georges Loiseau, Médan, July 25, 1902)

15

16

13 to 15. Backdrop Zola installed for portraiture.   16. Zola conversing with Georges Loiseau.

17

17. Self-portrait in front of the backdrop.
18. Zola examining a developer in a graduated beaker.   19 and 20. Notes on photography made by Zola, from among thirteen recently discovered pages.

18

It is always a good idea to develop too light. As soon as the outline of the face appears, the developing must be stopped. The picture will keep on developing while the stirring continues. Developing too much too soon will make the proofs black. By working with an under-developed negative, one ends up with a print à la Rembrandt. In reality, it should always be too light, particularly with sanguines. When those are over-developed, they end up too thick, too dark. It is imperative that they remain bright.

Work with half the luminous plate, the one with the yellow label, for cloudy September afternoons between 2 and 3, with intermittent sunshine. I have placed the backdrop facing the sarcophagus at six or seven meters, and I set it for 8 to 10 seconds with the number three diaphragm. Day in the studio. Carved faces—the eyes too much in the dark. The backdrop should perhaps be moved further back. With the plates with blue labels 5 minutes setting at most is necessary. Must work always keeping in mind the photogenic elements of a face.

him to photograph himself and shoot a group at a distance; he developed and printed his own negatives; he tried out different kinds of paper—the blues and greens, the Pan paper then in fashion, even platinum paper, which was less apt to age and which, thanks to its velvety grays and blacks, brought a new aesthetic quality to the photographic print.

For the exigencies of portraiture, Zola set up a neutral-colored backcloth out-of-doors. And if his study of compositions and still lifes (in which he described the play of light as "that which draws as well as colors—it is life itself") appears a bit casual, Zola showed his preference for motion, everyday scenes, and natural subjects.

Zola pointed his lens at all angles: sometimes, he used a horizontal platform, at others, a vertical one. He went out on his terrace to take pictures; he climbed to the top of the Trocadéro or up two flights of the brand-new Eiffel Tower. One of the last cameras he acquired—the Kodak Panoramic—allowed him to use an unusual format: 3.5 by 12 inches.

His manner, his working methods—one could say his style—in no way yielded to the habits of the time. He never made any touch-ups, not even in the portraits; he refused to use then-popular props, such as the bench, handrail, or stand. Zola tried out different formats (up to 12 by 16 inches!) and he used both plates and film (the latter had just made its appearance). He took snapshots as well as poses of various durations, and he wielded his camera

21. Enlarged, a 2.5-by-3.5-inch print reveals this detail: Zola, the Jumelle Carpentier, and the children on the steps of the Indochinese Pavilion at the World's Fair of 1900.

22. Cameras in Dr. François Émile-Zola's collection. (Photo Jacques Robert)

A. Brichaut camera, made of mahogany and copper with a black wood frame.

B. Folding Pocket Kodak no. 3.

C. A leather bag for the frames.

D. A 1902 Vest Pocket camera.

E. A Vest Pocket Kodak that dates from 1912 and belonged to Jacques Émile-Zola, the writer's son, together with its case and tripod.

F. An Eastman Kodak Cartridge no. 5.

G. A Jumelle Carpentier.

H. Another Jumelle Carpentier (in its case), the property of Jean-Claude Le Blond.

I. A box of dry silver gelatin–bromide plates with the label "A. Lumière et ses Fils."

J. A cloth satchel containing frames.

The following is a catalog of the photographic equipment Zola used, which is in the collection of Dr. François Émile-Zola. This collection includes a number of accessories, such as tripods, printing frames, and satchels, but we can presume that Zola's darkrooms contained much more. Jean-Claude Le Blond has, in fact, recently found an anonymous notebook with this inscription on its cover: "21, rue de Bruxelles—Copie du procès-verbal Zola" (Copy of the Zola proceedings). The notebook documents the sale of the property in the writer's home that took place shortly after his death in five separate sessions on March 9 through 13, 1903.

The following objects were sold the first day:

Kodak Panoramic	61 francs
4 printing frames and 4 developing dishes	9
A parcel of photographic utensils	11
6 developing dishes	27
A parcel of photographic plates	6
Photographic utensils	29
Camera obscura and 3 double plate holders	47
Lens	80
Enlarger	165
Lens	16
Camera without lens	125
Stand	52
Lens and vignetting card	44

M. J. Bourdon, director of the Center for Information and Scientific and Technical Documentation of the Kodak-Pathé Company, was able to furnish interesting details

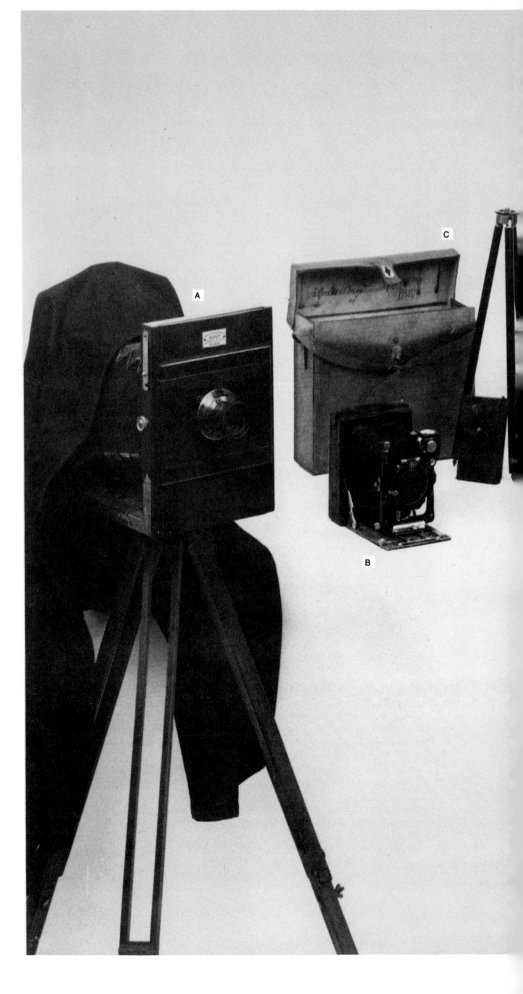

D

E

F

H

I

G

J

on some of the cameras in Dr. Émile-Zola's collection.

The Detective Nadar, *which dates from 1887, could take 3.5-by-4.75-inch plates or could be equipped with an Eastman Walker bobbin frame.*

The Kodak Panoramic no. 4, *made in 1889, was capable of taking 3.5-by-12-inch negatives with 100 mm film; it covered an angle of 142°.*

The Cartridge Kodak no. 5, *which came out in 1901, could take 12 5-by-7-inch pictures (format 115).*

The Folding Pocket Kodak no. 3, *which dates from 1900, took 12 3.25-by-4.25-inch (8.5-by-10.5-cm) pictures (format 118) and was equipped with a rectilinear lens.*

The Jumelle Carpentier, *made in 1892, took 1.75-by-2.25-inch pictures and had two lenses: one was an aplanatic, the other a viewfinder, which formed the image on a focusing screen that one could see through a red window fitted to the back of the camera.*

L. Joux's Steno-jumelle *dates from 1894: its double anastigmatic Goerz lens had a focal length of 3.25 to 51.25 inches and a five-speed drop shutter; it could take 18 pictures on a 3.5-by-4.75-inch plate.*

Mürer's Express, *dating from 1900, was of the Box type and took 2.5-by-3.5-inch pictures.*

in all types of weather: in the sun, in the rain and snow, even at night.

Later, Paul Valéry, opposing the realism of Letters to that of the lens, would say about photography that it "forces us to stop describing that which, of itself, inscribes itself." In contrast, we know the importance that Degas attached to photography and the influence it had on his art. "My visual memory has a power, an extraordinary vividness," Zola asserted. "When I evoke the objects which I've seen, I see them again the way they really are, with their lines, their forms, their colors, their odors, their sounds. It is the ultimate materialization: the sun which illuminated them almost dazzles me."

Life in Médan

In the spring of 1878, Zola traveled through the valley of the Seine downriver from Paris. He was looking for a house to rent so he could both finish *Les Rougon-Macquart* in a peaceful setting and provide a place where his mother could rest. Nevertheless, Zola did not want to go too far from Paris, since the World's Fair would open on the first of May.

About 40 kilometers from the capital, he discovered a house "hidden in a nest of greenery and separated from the rest of the hamlet by a magnificent row of trees" (From Paul Alexis, *Émile Zola, notes d'un ami* [Paris: Georges Charpentier, éditeur, 1882]). A For Sale sign hung on the door. Zola hesitated for a few days. At last, for the sum of nine thousand francs, he made up his mind to buy this "rabbit warren." "Literature," he wrote to Gustave Flaubert, "paid for this modest country retreat which has the merit of being far away from any resort and of not having a single *bourgeois* in the neighborhood" (*Émile Zola, Correspondance,* tome III [Paris: Presses de l'Université de Montréal/Editions du CNRS, 1982]).

This "rabbit warren" was in fact a two-story house surrounded by a narrow garden. Fifty meters below it ran the westward train, the one in *La Bête humaine*.

In Médan, Zola would write the most important parts of *Les Rougon-Macquart*: *Nana, Germinal,* and *La Terre,* as well as *Les Trois Villes* and two of the *Quatre Évangiles*. Until his children reached school age, he would spend

23. Edmond de Goncourt, by Nadar. (Photographic Archives. © SPADEM) 24. Guy de Maupassant. 25. Paul Cézanne, self-portrait. 26. Zola, with the house in Médan in the background.

nearly eight months of the year in Médan, from May–June to the end of December.

In 1877 *L'Assommoir* had appeared in bookstores. This novel of Parisian mores was the first to use slang, and its serialization in newspapers created such an uproar that it was nearly suspended. The following year, the battle was on; once more Zola was the prey of journalists, satirists, and caricaturists. Very rapidly, *L'Assommoir* attained thirty-five printings, and the magnanimous editor Charpentier tore up the contract that had made him the sole beneficiary of the book's success and gave the author a percentage of the sales. It was a fortune: 18,500 francs! as much revenue in a few months as the total from all his previous books.

Zola was more than busy in Médan. He had decided to build brick and cement additions on each side of the simple house and to be both architect and contractor for the construction. From then on, the house grew "at a pace equal to that of the work." The neighboring fields were bought up and transformed into wooded parks; stables and chicken coops were built, as were a greenhouse and, on the island (also partially bought), a chalet for which Mme Zola would lay the first stone.

While Émilie, the writer's mother, was astonished by all the luxury, Zola settled himself into the immense studio in the square tower, where medieval armor mingled with Japanese curios. From a large bay window, the view extended from the heights of the Hautil to the confluence

24

27

27. The village of Médan. On the right, behind the row of trees, is Zola's property.
28. Another view of the village, with Zola's property in the middle.

"Médan is a very small village of, at the most, two hundred souls on the left bank of the Seine in between Poissy and Triel. There is a high and a low Médan: that is to say of the few peasant cottages that some of them are strung along the road to Triel—halfway up a pretty hillside unevenly planted here and there with a bunch of walnut trees—while the others appear to have slid to the bottom of the slope, down to the embankment of the railroad track, which runs west and parallel, at this place, to the Seine, a few hundred meters or so from the shore." (Paul Alexis, Émile Zola, notes d'un ami, 1882)

of the Oise and Seine—the latter flowing right below, next to the railroad tracks. After taking a walk in the park with his dogs, the writer worked from nine o'clock until the moment the bell rang for lunch. In the afternoon, stretched out on his sofa, he took a nap or read the books he had received. At the height of the season, guests might go by carriage to fetch friends at the neighboring station or play boule, billiards, or better yet croquet, which was then in fashion. After piling into the *Nana*—a rowboat brought from Bezons by Maupassant and so baptized "because nearly everyone spends some time on her"—they would go to the Paradou on the island for tea (quote from Armande Lanoux, *Bonjour, Monsieur Zola* [Paris: Amiot-Dumont, 1964]).

Mme Zola, married to the author since the eve of the war of 1870, presided over the little world of servants and workmen, who were particularly numerous during the construction period. She paid the wages on Saturday night, oversaw the maintenance of the property, and organized the daily bill of fare. Zola, according to Maupassant, ate "like three ordinary novelists," and the Médan house was always wide open to friends.

Zola, who acted as the head of the school of Naturalism, would entertain men of letters (such as Edmond de Goncourt, Octave Mirbeau, and the contributors to the *Soirées de Médan*, Paul Alexis, Henry Céard, Léon Hennique, J. K. Huysmans, and Guy de Maupassant); musicians such

29. A street in Médan.   30. The original house flanked by the new constructions. On the left is the "Germinal" tower (the open window on the second floor is the linen room, where Jeanne Rozerot worked); to the right is the square tower, also known as "Nana," where the writer had his studio beneath the terrace; hidden partly by trees, on the right, is the "Charpentier" pavilion, reserved for friends.

"The little house looked like a farm and the garden was as big as a handkerchief. A few weeks later, the masons, the painters, the upholsterers arrived to begin the first renovations. They haven't left since!" (Paul Alexis, Émile Zola, notes d'un ami)

29

30

31

31. The view from Zola's studio of the
Seine and the heights of Hautil. The railroad track, for the Paris–Le Havre line, is
hidden. 32. The Paradou on the island.
Zola is on the balcony. "On September
27th, 1880, I laid the first stone of this
house" (Mme Alexandrine Zola). Zola
added, "I was present when my dear wife
laid the first stone." These texts are pre-
served in an iron box that was sealed inside
the wall. (The chalet was demolished in
1935.)   33. The Seine and the island of
Platais (a large part of which Zola bought).

32

33

as Alfred Bruneau, who got the inspiration for a lyrical drama from *Le Rêve*; and painters like Antoine Guillemet and Paul Cézanne. Guillemet was the one who first introduced Zola to Cézanne's painting. Cézanne went to Médan several times, and it was there that he sketched a *Triomphe de la femme*; he also planted his easel on the island for a *Portrait de Mme Zola prenant le thé dans son jardin* (Portrait of Mme Zola having tea in her garden), which the artist subsequently destroyed in a rage after a remark by Guillemet. And if Zola did not leave us a portrait of his fellow student from Aix and companion from L'Estaque, it is because their relationship cooled somewhat after the publication of *L'Oeuvre*, for Cézanne thought he recognized himself in the character of Claude Lantier, the painter so taken by perfection that his work becomes powerless. And also because, in 1886, of course, Zola had not yet taken up photography.

34. The dining room.   35. The writer in his studio.   36. The monumental fireplace.
37. The kitchen.

34

35

36

"The billiard room with its mosaic floor took up the entire surface of the big tower whose walls were cornered off on the sides of the garden and the Seine but formed right angles on the sides of the kitchen courtyard and the road. This room was very high, the beams on the ceiling were decorated with the arms of Médan and, perhaps, of Dourdan, according to Carnavalet's armorial sketches and with the winged lion of St. Mark found by Zola's Italian friend Cameron. A very large and high stone fireplace occupied the center of the wall facing the entrance.

"To the left, toward the garden, and receiving the light of day filtered through huge modern windowpanes, stood a massive table covered with a thick cloth, on which rested a knick-knack shelf, desk utensils, some books. This, together with three or four chairs, and a sturdy armchair, upholstered in either cloth or leather, formed the intimate center of life." (Albert Laborde, from an interview compiled in 1969 by Henri Mitterand in Cahiers naturalistes, no. 38)

"In the dining room, the table could easily accommodate five to eight guests and we were even more numerous. Zola and his wife sat at the two extremities, he with his back to the garden. Each one of them sat in their own particular chair; they used silver goblets.

"Of the furniture in this room, paneled shoulder height in dark wood, I especially remember a small sort of sideboard, credenza style, in the corner against the garden wall, behind Zola and to his left, whose drawer contained the medicine Zola sometimes took at mealtimes. A sideboard in the opposite corner at a diagonal along the kitchen wall. . . . On four consoles fixed on each side of the kitchen door and on the interior sills of the windows facing the Seine, one could see the little ceramic statues of the four evangelists, Matthew, Mark, Luke, and John." (Albert Laborde, from Cahiers naturalistes)

"In front of the house, beyond the field separated from the garden by the railroad track, Zola sees from his windows the large ribbon of the Seine flowing toward Triel, then, an immense plain and some white villages on the distant hillsides and, above that, some woods crowning the heights." (Guy de Maupassant, Émile Zola)

"Here in the new studio, everything is immense. The dimensions fit for a painter of historical scenes. . . . A colossal fireplace where a tree could roast an entire sheep. In the back, a sort of alcove, itself as big as one of our little rooms in Paris, completely filled by a single sofa in which ten people could sleep comfortably. In the middle, a very big table. Finally, in front of the table, a large bay window providing a view of the Seine. I won't mention a sort of platform, built over the alcove or sofa, to which one gains access by a circular staircase: it's the library. The same staircase leads to the square terrace that takes up the entire roof of this new building, which can be seen from afar in the country and from which the panorama is splendid.

"From nine o'clock to one o'clock, seated in

38

front of his immense table, Zola works on one of his novels. Nulle dies sine linea *is the motto inscribed in gold letters on the hood of the fireplace." (Paul Alexis,* Émile Zola, notes d'un ami)

"I want to have a huge studio with beds everywhere and a terrace overlooking the countryside." (Zola to Gustave Flaubert, September 28, 1878)

"This immense studio is also hung with immense tapestries and cluttered with furniture from all different periods and different countries. Medieval armor, authentic or not, is placed side by side with strange Japanese furniture and graceful eighteenth-century objects." (Guy de Maupassant, Émile Zola)

"The kitchen was huge and one could guess

the importance of the room by its extreme cleanliness, by the arsenal of pans, utensils, pots that filled it. It smelled good and of good food. Provisions overflowed from the racks and the cupboards." (Zola, Germinal)

"The island metamorphosed, its chalet, the bushes, the lawn, all date from Nana. *The greenhouse with its rare flowers, the stables, the henhouses, where a nation of beasts swarm, it's* Pot-Bouille *that paid for them all." (Alfred Bruneau,* À L'Ombre d'un grand coeur, *1932)*

"We lunch merrily and afterward we go to the island where [Zola] is having a chalet built . . . which contains a large room all in pine with a monumental tile stove of beautiful simplicity and great taste." (Journal des Goncourt, *June 20, 1881)*

39

38. Lenôtre, a Médan servant, with the horse Bonhomme.   39. Alfred Bruneau in the carriage, driven by the coachman Jules.

40

40. The Zolas and the Charpentiers in the garden in Médan. On the ground, Desmoulin. 41. Bruneau, Henry Dutard, Charpentier, Mme Bruneau and her daughter, Mme Charpentier, Mme Zola. 42. Zola has replaced Charpentier, who probably took the photograph. 43. Around the sarcophagus in front of the Charpentier pavilion: Zola (as "The Thinker"), Bruneau, Albert and Élina Laborde, Mme Amélie Laborde. 44. Near Poissy, the play of light on the water.

41

42

43

45

45. The village of Médan as seen from Zola's terrace. 46. On the Médan road, Georges Charpentier (on the left) accompanied by Dutard and his wife, Jeanne, née Charpentier. 47. Panoramic view of Médan.

46

48

49

50

51

52

48. The outskirts of Médan.   49. Mme Amélie Laborde being taken to Médan on a quadricycle driven by her son, Albert. 50. Gaston Picq-Brière giving Albert Laborde a ride on his motorized quadricycle. 51. Mme Zola on her tricycle.   52. A young guest, the equilibrist Albert Laborde.   53. Zola lying in the hay.   54. Zola lying in the grass with Pinpin (September 20, 1895).   55. Élina Laborde, Mme Zola, Mme Amélie Laborde. Albert Laborde holds the bicycle, and Jules holds the reins.

53

54

56

56. Departure by train: Jeanne, the children, Mme Alexis.   57 and 58. The trains and barges that pass by the foot of Zola's property.

57

58

59

60

59. A barge passing in front of the island
and the chalet.   60. The port of Le Havre.
In March of 1889, Zola visited Le Havre
train station in search of documentation
for *La Bête humaine* and may have taken
this naturalistic photo of the harbor. (The
print was made from a positive found in
Zola's studio.)

A Second Family

Jeanne-Sophie-Adèle Rozerot was born April 14, 1867, in Rouvres-sous-Meilly in the Auxois. She was the second daughter of a miller who, when he was widowed, remarried and had to bring up a large family. Suffering from the loss of her mother, Jeanne often sought comfort from her maternal grandmother.

She was working as a seamstress when she was recommended to Mme Zola. Hired by her in May 1888, Jeanne accompanied the Zolas to Royan for the summer because Alexandrine could not do without her. And since Mme Zola was often indisposed and wished to remain alone, she sent her husband off on walks with the young girl. It was a "perpetual feast" for the writer, who was "experiencing a very productive working period, who [felt] wonderfully well and the way he did at twenty when he wanted to eat mountains" (*Le Docteur Pascal* [Paris: Georges Charpentier, éditeur, 1893]).

Jeanne was twenty-one years old; she had "light eyes, full lips, her delicate neck [was] especially satiny and round, her nape [was] shaded by stray locks of hair." He was twenty-seven years older than she. "It was monstrous," Zola would admit in *Le Docteur Pascal*, "but it was true enough, he was hungry for all that, filled with a devouring hunger for that youth, that flowerlike flesh that was so pure and that smelled so good."

On his return to Paris in October, Zola was unrecognizable; since the previous winter he had lost weight, trimmed

61. The region around Médan and Verneuil. 62 and 63. Jeanne Rozerot photographed by Pierre Petit. (The latter print was touched up with color.)

his beard, begun to dress more elegantly. He installed Jeanne on the fifth floor of 66, rue Saint-Lazare; from the rue Blanche side, her windows looked onto the square de la Trinité. A postcard, addressed to Jeanne ten years later from England, where he went into exile, probably commemorates the anniversary of the beginning of the couple's amorous relationship on December 11, 1888.

Their first child, Denise, was born at rue Saint-Lazare on September 20, 1889. "The sharing, this double life that I am forced to live, ends by filling me with despair," Zola wrote to Jeanne. To her he also confided, "I don't want to add remorse to our love." He did not have the courage to sacrifice Alexandrine.

Two years later, on September 25, 1891, their second child was born while Zola was traveling in the Pyrénées with Alexandrine. He learned of the birth through a brief personal ad placed in the *Figaro* by Henry Céard, which read: "Pheasant arrived fine." "Put pheasant for a boy, hen pheasant for a girl, like it had to do with an aviary," Zola had told his friend. Not long after, tipped off by an anonymous letter, Mme Zola rushed to rue Saint-Lazare, broke open a desk, and burned all her husband's letters.

"I did all I could to prevent anyone from going to your house," Zola wrote to Jeanne. "I am very unhappy. Do not despair." "I had the dream of making everyone around me happy," Zola wrote again. "But I see that that is impossible and I am the first one to be struck." Did he plan

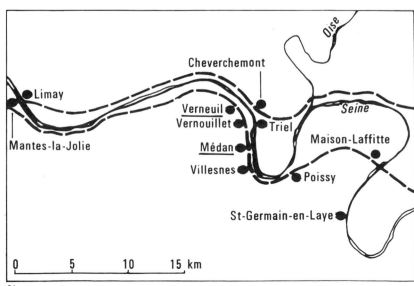

to give up Jeanne, or did he think of leaving Alexandrine? We do not know. "For weeks, months," he confided to a friend, "a storm has been raging inside me, a storm of desires and regrets." He particularly suffered over having to force Jeanne to live as a recluse; Jeanne, who inspired him with the plot of *Le Docteur Pascal* and to whom he would give a copy printed on Japanese vellum with this dedication: "To my beloved Jeanne, to my Clotilde, who gave me the royal banquet of her youth and who brought back my thirties by giving me the gift of my Denise and Jacques." Zola, who loved children, did not have any with Alexandrine.

In 1893, during the summer months, Jeanne and the children went to Cheverchemont near Triel, opposite, although slightly downriver, from Médan. Nevertheless, Zola complained of not being able to "play the good father to his children" more often. Since he could only rarely visit them on foot, he followed their games with the help of his binoculars from the terrace of his studio. "I must have your portrait, of all three of you, at this distant window from which I have so often watched you," he wrote to Jeanne. (He would, in fact, have a painting done of that scene.) Two months later, from London during the Congrès de la Presse (Congress of the Press), at which four thousand people hailed him, he again confessed to Jeanne: "I am telling you this, my sweet Jeanne, because at that moment I was thinking of you. Yes, in a little corner of France,

62

63

64

64. Jeanne and Zola in 1893. Whatever talent this anonymous photograph may reveal, it seems flagrantly academic when compared with Zola's natural compositions. One hardly recognizes Jeanne as the same woman in both.

there were three beings who were very dear to me, and though they were in the shade, they shared in my glory no less. I want *you* and my two darlings to have your part. One day, they will surely have to be my children for the whole world so that then, everything that happens here will also be for you. I want them to share the name of their father!"

During the following summers, Jeanne and the children moved to Verneuil, to a house with a large garden closer to Médan. Thus, the young woman would be able to meet with the writer, to whom she appeared like an impressionistic type of poetic fantasy, which finds its expression in *Le Docteur Pascal*: "She, shaded a bit by her parasol, bloomed happily under this bath of light like a plant in broad daylight."

Soon, Zola went every day by bicycle to visit his second family for tea. From then on, nothing would stop him from going, according to Denise, "neither bad weather, nor tremendous heat, not even a physical ailment." Zola had made peace with Alexandrine. Later, she would even become attached to the children. (After the death of her husband, Mme Zola would make friends with Jeanne, authorize the children to bear the name Émile-Zola, and attend to their education.)

Jeanne brought up the children to worship their father. "She gave my father her fervent love, which was filled with both admiration and tenderness," Denise wrote. "But their relationship, which resembled that of the most united couple, caused those two beings to suffer from the lie since they respected the truth like an idol." Zola, for his part, confided to Jeanne: "I would have wanted to give your youth a few pleasures and not to have forced you to live like a recluse: I would have been so happy to be young with you, to rejuvenate myself with your youth, instead of which, it is I who age you, who continually make you sad."

For, in Verneuil, visits were rare and made only by a few intimate friends, such as the Alexises, who were neighbors. Paul Alexis (whom Zola had dubbed Trublot in *Au bonheur des dames*) was one of the six of the *Soirées de Médan*; he was Zola's most loyal friend as well as his compatriot from Aix; he had followed the writer throughout his entire career; he was Jacques's godfather, and he regarded Jeanne highly. Later, during the Dreyfus affair, Alexis would again give his support to Zola. Zola would be greatly affected by the sudden death of Alexis in 1901.

In Verneuil, Zola's camera captured Jeanne at her daily tasks: sewing, arranging flowers, supervising her children's homework, relaxing with a book, or assuming a slightly languid pose to play the mandolin. It was during the summer of 1897 that the writer, not satisfied to photograph Jeanne from every angle and in all her finery—with or without her hat or veil, with a boa wrapped around her neck, with her hair undone in the guise of a gypsy, and even in old-fashioned *déshabillé*—set about a veritable photographic reportage of the life of his children. Thus, he composed an album which he entitled "Denise and Jacques, A True Story, by Émile Zola." He had it bound elegantly and embellished it with a dedication to Jeanne.

During another summer, that of 1899, Zola gave Denise and Jacques the bicycles he had promised them during his exile in England. From then on, parents and children could move without restraint in the Verneuil woods, in the valley of the Seine, as far as Mantes, or upriver toward Maisons-Lafitte, going past Poissy, Triel, Limay. On these outings, the novelist took photos of the villages, the churches, the bridges that span the valley, the stretch of white roads, the towns, whose streets were drowsy with summer heat or animated by the presence of a market, such as the one at Mantes. They passed harnessed teams and farmers' carts; they followed the Seine all the way to the banks of Saint-Germain.

Now Zola was well established in his double life: he went to Verneuil openly, and, in Paris, he divided his time between the rue de Bruxelles, where he worked in the morning and lunched with Alexandrine, and Jeanne's home, where he spent the afternoon. The homes of the two "wives" contained some of the same objects, such as the garden chairs—exactly identical—which one can see in the photos of Médan as well as in those of Verneuil.

"How I did love this father who dedicated his hours of

leisure to us," Denise would write later, "how much more would I have loved him still had I known his secret distress!" And, further along: "We were happy, we loved each other dearly, parents and children. Nothing seemed capable of diminishing this happiness." Nothing but the brutal death of the writer on an autumn night in 1902. A few days earlier, they had celebrated the children's birthdays.

65. Émile Zola with Jeanne Rozerot, their daughter, Denise, and their son, Jacques.

66

66. Jeanne on her way to meet Zola on the road from Verneuil. "She, shaded a bit by her parasol, bloomed happily under this bath of light like a plant in broad daylight." (Zola, *Le Docteur Pascal*) 67. Zola's goodbye to Jeanne. 68. Jeanne. 69. The children.

Our mother lived only for Zola and her children. She accepted the life of a recluse, she saw
only a few intimate friends. . . . She provided
Zola with that great tenderness that his in-
tellect required; she welcomed him to a peaceful hearth, far from the outside bustle, with
her beautiful smile, her clear eyes, her lovely
mouth, her admiring love. She had an indis-
putable influence on his work: one cannot but
recognize it in Marianne and Josine; it is her,
the ever brave and cheerful mother."

In July 1901, Zola was very much affected
by the sudden death of Alexis, his great and
faithful friend who had followed his entire
career as a battling writer, during the painful
part of the Affair, he who was a compatriot
at Aix and who saw eye to eye with him in
literary discussions. Alexis was also my brother's godfather; his family and ours were one;
from 1888 on, he knew all about Zola's moral
struggles and he held Jeanne Rozerot in great
esteem." (Denise Le Blond-Zola, *Émile Zola
raconté par sa fille*)

70

"An indulgent father, he never punished us; only once, in England, did he get angry with my brother, who was very finicky about food; another time, it was with me, in Verneuil: he wanted to photograph me on his bicycle, which Jacques held; I was dying of fear that I would fall and I started to cry; the photo was taken by my father, who had lost his patience. . . . I remember something else, the arrival of a parrot from Senegal that my father had received with several others from Léon Hennique, who had a brother in the colonies. This parrot lived with us a long time; greedy and mean, he often bit Zola's fingers if he wasn't paying attention while he was putting bits of banana in between the bars of the cage."
(Denise Le Blond-Zola, Émile Zola raconté par sa fille)

70 and 71. Teatime.

72

73

74

75

72 to 75. The children's games. Note, in photograph 72, the marker Zola had placed on the ground.   76. Zola in Verneuil.

77

77 and 78. The children's games. Most of the photographs that illustrate these pages were taken during the summer of 1897 and are part of the album Zola made and entitled *A True Story*.   79. A game of croquet with the Triouleyres (summer 1897). "Triouleyre was our great friend, the companion of our games. He became a child again to please us." (Denise Le Blond-Zola, *Émile Zola raconté par sa fille*)

80

80 and 81. In the Verneuil garden.

82

83

82 and 83. Denise and Jacques with their bicycles.   84 to 87. The summer of 1899, Zola gave the family bicycles, and there were long rides through the Verneuil woods.   88 and 89. The rendezvous.

84

85

"*From then on, we spent the summer in Verneuil, very close to Médan. Zola had bought a bicycle. When he had made peace with his wife and when he could divide his days between her and us, he came every day after lunch. Nothing could have stopped him, neither bad weather, nor tremendous heat, not even a physical ailment.*" (Denise Le Blond-Zola, Émile Zola raconté par sa fille)

86

87

88

90. The woods around Verneuil, Denise and Jeanne at center with a parasol.

91

92

91. The rue Galande, which, in Triel, runs underneath the church. 92. A street in Mantes. 93. Jeanne and the children in the Verneuil woods.

The Trip to Italy

On his first trip to Italy in 1892, Zola had stayed in Genoa only two days. This time, he planned to spend six weeks in Italy (from October 31 to December 15, 1894), in the company of his wife. By his own avowal, the novelist wanted to get to know "Rome as quick as the wind, the monuments in three days, her mores in four, consecrate three days to Leon XIII and the Vatican, and three days for the economic and social conditions."

Welcomed to the capital by Attilio Luzzato and Count Bertolelli, director and manager respectively of the *Tribuna*—the newspaper that had published the translation of *Les Rougon-Macquart*—the couple stayed at the Grand Hotel. The very day of his arrival, Zola paid a visit to the French ambassador, Albert Billot, as well as to Lefebvre de Behaine, the ambassador to the Vatican, to whom he had an introduction from Edmond de Goncourt. In vain, Zola would try to obtain a private audience with Leo XIII (his book *Lourdes* had just been put on the Index). To make up for that disappointment, he would be received at the Quirinal on December 1 by King Humbert I and three days later Alexandrine would be received by Queen Margaret.

Zola visited Rome systematically—the gardens, the poor sections, and the Roman countryside. He met with politicians, princesses, prelates; he attended a mass at St. Peter's; he saw the principal churches and spent two days exploring the ruins of the ancient city, where he took photographs—

especially of the excavations being undertaken in the Forum.

From November 23 to 28, Zola was in Naples, where he was met by the writer Vittorio Picca and where a banquet for two hundred people was given in his honor. He visited Pompeii, climbed Vesuvius, and took a boat to Capri before he returned to the capital.

Once he had put together the documentation that would enable him to write *Rome* the following year, Zola left for Florence on December 5. He spent two days there, then went on to Venice, where he was received by his cousin, the magistrate Carlo Zola. During a reception, Zola made a toast "to this bewitching city," where his father was born and "of which he might have been the child." It is strange that Zola did not leave a photographic testimony of the three days he spent in the aqueous city. He did, however, take snapshots of the Piazza del Campo in Siena, a city that he did not mention in his account of his Italian journey. The journey came to an end in Milan, setting of Zola's meeting with the writers Giacosa and Elice Cameroni.

During this sojourn in the country of his ancestors (where he was received "like a native son, an illustrious son who is acclaimed and fought over like a distinguished guest"), Zola paid little attention, so it seems, to the announcement of the arrest on November 1, 1894, of a certain Captain Alfred Dreyfus on charges that he was a German spy.

95

94. The welcome in Rome.   95. The Arch
of Septimius Severus; to the right, the
Temple of Antoninus and Faustina. (The
print was made from a positive found in
Zola's studio.)

96

97

98

99

100

96. Rome.   97. On the left, the columns
of the Temple of Vespasian; to the right,
those of the Temple of Saturn; in the
center, the Church of San Luca and Santa
Martina. 98. Students from a Salesian
school.   99. In the street.   100. A funeral
procession in a street in Rome.

Exile in England

On February 23, 1898, Zola was condemned to a year in prison for slandering the army in his brave defense of Alfred Dreyfus. He appealed. On April 2, the Court of Appeals overturned the judgment; in the meantime, the War Council, which had acquitted Major Esterhazy, lodged a complaint against Zola. Once again, a campaign of calumny was launched against the writer; a journalist—with the help of old and distorted archival material—went so far as to attack the reputation of Zola's father, provoking a heated counterreaction from Zola in *L'Aurore*.

Meanwhile, in Versailles on July 18, the judgment of February was confirmed by default. From that moment on, there could be no more recourse in the courts. Not daring to return home, Zola went to the home of his editor, Charpentier, where he met with his lawyers and some of his friends. He was tired and disillusioned, but Georges Clemenceau and Fernand Labori persuaded him to choose exile rather than prison. Zola, who at first wouldn't hear of it, let himself be persuaded. He sent for his wife, who had remained at rue de Bruxelles. Alexandrine arrived; she didn't dare bring a suitcase for fear of arousing the suspicion of the policemen stationed around the writer's home.

"The 18th of July will remain the awful date in my life, the one on which I bled all my blood," Zola confessed in *Pages d'exil*. "It [was] on the 18th of July that, surrendering to tactical necessities and listening to the advice of my brothers-in-arms who led the same battle with me for the honor of France, I had to tear myself away from everything that I loved, from all the habits of my heart and soul."

On the very night of the verdict, Zola, gloomy and alone, took the train from the Gare du Nord. He traveled incognito, with "only a nightshirt and a few other small objects folded inside a newspaper" (*Pages d'exil*, in Nottingham French Studies, Vol. 3, no. 1 [May 1964]). Forewarned by Desmoulin, Jeanne stayed in Verneuil with the children. "When I saw the lights of Calais go out in the night from the boat, my eyes became filled with tears," Zola wrote to his lawyer Fernand Labori, on July 19. "Ah! The abominable thing, one day I will speak of my heartbreak. But truth and justice must triumph" (*La Grande Revue* [May 1929]).

Early the next morning, Zola arrived at Victoria Station. Following Clemenceau's instructions, he hailed a carriage to take him to the Grosvenor Hotel. The coachman was astounded, but Zola, who did not speak a word of English, insisted; so the driver deposited the writer 50 meters away, at the door of the hotel.

Since he did not have any luggage, Zola had to pay a pound in advance. He registered under the name M. Pascal and spent the first two nights of his exile at the Grosvenor. On the twenty-first, he was taken to Wimbledon by F. W. Wareham, a jurist who happened to be a friend and neighbor of Ernest Vizetelly, the English translator and publisher of *Les Rougon-Macquart*. On his arrival, Zola had written

PREUVES ÉCRASANTES de la TRAHISON

Appel à tous les Français. — Mort aux Traîtres !

L'HONNEUR DE L'ARMÉE — L'INDIGNATION DE NOS SOLDATS

INFAMES MACHINATIONS

Le Syndicat Dreyfus   A bas les juifs! — D'où vient l'argent

LES RÉVÉLATIONS DE LA FEMME VOILÉE

Un Complot de faussaires.   A Mazas ! — Les aveux du traître

Défense impossible Témoignages irrécusables Les vols	rer-Kestner, les Mathieu Dreyfus, tous les avocats, tous les journalistes payés par la caisse	vérité du général Billot a, de plus, le tort de venir un peu tard... ce que l'on n'admet que	échéance la chute du ministère. A cette tragédie, la partie comique ne pouvait manquer.	nant à la police française et ayant eu des relations avec un membre de la famille Dreyfus.	nier membre encore sain d vieux sol gaulois. Les magistrats du consei

to Vizetelly: "Don't tell a soul and especially not a newspaper that I am in London. And be so kind as to come and see me tomorrow morning, Wednesday, at eleven o'clock at the Grosvenor Hotel." At the meeting, Zola found both his translator and two friends from Paris, Fernand Desmoulin and Bernard Lazare. Lazare brought the news that the prefect of police in Paris had sent out his agents in search of the fugitive. The stations, the harbors, the frontiers were all under surveillance. Zola had reportedly been seen everywhere: in Lucerne, in Spa, in Antwerp, in Hamburg, in The Hague; he had been glimpsed in Switzerland, in Norway, and even in Verneuil. Monsieur Beauchamp (Zola's new pseudonym), constantly afraid of being recognized, moved to the Oatlands Park Hotel on July 22. The hotel, in Weybridge, a little village in Surrey, close to the Thames and about a dozen miles from the capital, was also an old royal residence. It had sheltered King Louis-Philippe after the revolution of 1848, and it was surrounded by vast gardens. Zola registered under another new name, Rogers. "I want to settle somewhere and not move again," he announced.

Soon, the writer found a house in the neighborhood to rent for four weeks. The furnished house was called Penn. Zola moved in on August 1, and the very next day, he wrote: "First day in the little house. In the morning, early, while the sun was on the facade, I took a picture of it [Desmoulin had gotten him a camera a few days be-

102

103

101. The press attacks Dreyfus. 102. The captain's degradation. 103. Colonel Picquart, the very model of the scrupulous officer, as photographed by Zola.

fore]. . . . And, since I had not gone out, we [Desmoulin and he] went, at around nine o'clock, as far as Walton, by the Oatlands road . . . and all the while, along lovely straight roads, bordered by giant trees. There are endless parks with large lawns of the darkest green, of a majestic silence." And further along: "This little house, with its light colors, its furniture of such a special style, its childish knick-knacks, its airy windows, tells us how far away we are from France."

Those lovely straight roads—Zola and Violette Vizetelly (his sixteen-year-old interpreter) would soon walk along them with Jacques and Denise. For, on August 11, Jeanne and the children arrived, to stay until mid-October. In turn, Mme Zola arrived October 30 and stayed until December 5. Then Jeanne returned for fifteen days in the spring. But the novelist was inconsolable over the death of his Pinpin. ("I cried about it like a child. . . . Those kinds of things are ridiculous, I know.") He tried to remember whether, on the morning of his departure for exile, he had taken the dog in his arms "to kiss him the way [he] always did" (*Pages d'exil*).

On August 27, Zola left Penn to settle in Summerfield (where he would spend six weeks), in a larger house surrounded by a big garden "with wild grass and with its hole, no doubt an old sand quarry, that has been transformed into a flower garden" (*Pages d'exil*). It was there that, a few days later, the news of Colonel Henry's suicide would reach him.

During that autumn, Zola took long walks to the neighboring villages of Chertsey, Cobham, Byfleet, Shepperton, and Windsor, where he took the children. In his notes, he mentioned "the admirable weather they had, the days spent in the garden, under such clear and gentle sunshine." Thanks to his rediscovered photographs (on whose backs appears his well-defined handwriting), we can reconstruct the novelist's life during his exile; Jeanne's presence had interrupted his journal entries for a while. After spending a few days at Bailey's Hotel in South Kensington, Zola settled at the Queen's Hotel in Upper Norwood, not far from the celebrated Crystal Palace. The palace, built for the World's Fair of 1851, was where, in 1893, Zola had attended a banquet given in his honor. The neighborhood was peaceful; one saw imposing houses but never their inhabitants. Zola was bored during that long winter: "Here, I am in a desert. I don't see anyone, my life continues without a distraction, without an event. I work, that's all." In another letter, he announced that his "decision was made not to tell anyone anything and to return one fine morning. The solitude I am in is beginning to drive me mad." On June 3, 1899, the court unanimously annulled the judgment against Captain Dreyfus. Two days later, Zola was back in Paris: "Soon, it will be eleven months since I left France. For eleven months, I have imposed upon myself the most complete exile, a retreat that was totally unknown. . . . It is finished, and I return since the truth is out, since justice is done."

104. A caricature of Zola published by *La Patrie* (January 16, 1898) with the intent of confounding those who took Dreyfus's defense.   105. Zola's famous letter to the president of the Republic, published in *L'Aurore* on January 13, 1898.   106. A session at Zola's trial: this one was devoted to the deposition of General Mercier.

108

107. Jeanne and the children at the window of Penn.   108. Mme Zola at the window of the Queen's Hotel.

109

"I work very regularly in the morning, I go out sometimes in the afternoon on my bicycle for a short outing. I go to Walton or to Weybridge, the two little villages in between which I live. I took some photographs of these two regions from the banks of the Wey and from the banks of the Thames. They are, I repeat, charming regions, some superb roads bordered by large parks and by beautiful trees."

"In my notes, also this recollection of my entire daily life at Summerfield, the walks to Chertsey, Cobham, Byfleet, Shepperton, Windsor. . . . The admirable weather we had, the days spent in the garden, in the clear and gentle sunshine. . . . The photographs I took a bit here and there and everywhere." (Zola, Pages d'exil)

110

109. The house opposite the Queen's Hotel.
110. The Walton Bridge.

111

112

111. A milk cart. 112. A hearse. 113 and 114. The neighborhood around the Crystal Palace.

115

"What strikes me most of all is the need to agglomerate, to squeeze together, one against the other. For the houses of the poor, the workmen's houses in the suburbs, nothing is more typical than this formation by swarms, by juxtaposition of cells, all of them alike. Streets, entire neighborhoods, are thus made up of little houses, stuck one against the other, identical. It would seem that the Phalanstère has been realized, the dream of our communists has been put into practice." (Zola, Pages d'exil)

116

115 and 116. The neighborhood around
the Crystal Palace.

117

117. Street scene near the Crystal Palace.
118 and 119. In London, as in Médan,
Zola showed a keen interest in trains.

Zola's Paris

Zola's Paris was no longer that of Balzac. The prefect Haussmann had totally transformed its appearance. Meanwhile, the elegant neighborhoods, adhering to some mysterious law that can be observed in several European capitals, continued to spread westward, chasing away the market gardens and the farms with their cows.

One after the other, the department stores, those modern temples of commerce which Zola celebrated in *Au bonheur des dames*, opened their doors. It was a time of a stable franc, of quick income and easy women; a time of Franco-Russian friendship and of duels, of "the eye fixed on the blue line of the Vosges" and of café-theaters. But the end of the century was also a time of political and financial scandals and of harshly quelled strikes, the time of the Dreyfus affair, and finally a time in which three plagues were prevalent—absinthe, tuberculosis, and syphilis. For, if charity sales and the slow and expensive construction of the Sacré-Coeur bought a good conscience for the well-to-do, the fact remained that Parisians had, perhaps, never been so rich as well as so poor at the same time. Also, in many places, Zola's Paris was still Eugène Sue's.

Today, it may be astonishing to see a kind of divorce between the "subjects" that interested Zola the photographer and the preoccupations of Zola the novelist in, for example, *L'Assommoir*. The photographer spent much time strolling down the alleys of the Tuileries or in the Luxembourg, the Parc de Monceau, the Buttes-Chaumont or

120

the Bois de Boulogne, and if he seemed to linger a bit in the place Clichy (he was not insensitive to its picturesqueness, especially in the rain), it was no doubt because he lived nearby. Still, it is difficult to fault this enlightened amateur photographer for his lack of interest in the Paris of the working class, inasmuch as his literary work was already written, and in it he had said precisely what he had to say about that milieu.

Nonetheless, at a time when photographs had not yet appeared in newspapers and remained confined to family albums, Zola's great merit was to have understood photography's role as a witness. Only later would a public place be found for these scenes "taken from life," these "snapshots," which were now possible thanks to improvements in the lenses and plates as well as, of course, the reduction in the weight of cameras.

121

122

120. The private house on the rue de Bruxelles where Zola lived from 1890 until his death. The stairs. 121. Zola in his study. 122. The place Clichy, seen from the enlarged part of the rue de Clichy. A few steps away is the rue de Bruxelles.

123

124

123. The place Clichy, seen from the corner of the rue d'Amsterdam.   124. The place Prosper-Goubaux and the avenue de Villiers; to the left, the boulevard de Courcelles.

125

125. The big boulevards in the rain.
126. The place Prosper-Goubaux and the
avenue de Villiers; on the right, the rue
de Levis.   127. The boulevard des Batig-
nolles and the rue de Rome.

126

128

129

128. Horse teams on the large central alley of the Parc Monceau. "The carriages that passed one another there were as numerous as on a boulevard." (Zola, *La Curée*)
129. Sweeping the alleys in the park.

130

130. Panoramic photograph of the avenue
du Bois. In the foreground is Zola's shadow.
131. The dock with boats for hire in the
Bois de Boulogne.   132. Under Jeanne's
watchful eye, Jacques and Denise feed the
swans on the lower lake of the Grand Lac.

131

133

133. A bicycle being transported on a quadricycle. The Arc de Triomphe is in the background.   134. The Printemps Department Stores, seen from the apartment Jeanne Rozerot occupied on the fourth floor of the rue du Havre.   135. A tugboat and a barge on the Seine.

134

136. Gare Saint-Lazare: Le Havre court-yard.

"All winter long, I went to Saint-Lazare Station, I wandered around the western track, looking, talking, going home with my pockets filled with notes." (Zola, Letter to J. van Santen Kolff, 1889, regarding La Bête humaine)

137

137. The place Clichy. One can imagine
Zola finishing his peregrinations through
Paris and returning home. "The coachmen
were immobile, stiffened in their frozen
coats. . . . In the snow, one by one, other
carriages advanced with difficulty. Cotton-
wool stifled the noise." (Zola, *Une Page
d'amour*)

The World's Fair
of 1900

The World's Fair of 1900 opened in a France happy with President Loubet. From now on, the Church would rally around the Republic. Dreyfus had just been pardoned, and the *métro* had been declared a public utility. Like the other nations on the Continent, France was experiencing prodigious technical and scientific advances, with the invention of the internal combustion engine, the telephone, the discoveries of radium by the Curies, the antirabies vaccine by Louis Pasteur, and Jules-Henri Poincaré's mathematical laws. It had become possible to record the human voice, pictures, and motion; Clément Ader had conquered gravity, balloons were dirigible, bicycles rolled on tires, and the automobile (before 1900) broke 100 kilometers an hour—albeit for one kilometer, and with a launched departure. The gas mantle was invented at the same time that electric light began to be used. And finally, France had acquired a colonial empire.

Spread over about 280 acres, the fair of 1900 included all the area occupied by the four preceding fairs (1855, 1867, 1878, and 1889). Its perimeter was traversed by two new methods of transport—a mobile platform and an electric train—and the eleven-year-old Eiffel Tower and the Trocadéro, twenty-two years old, attracted many visitors.

In 1878, Zola had broken his habit of taking seaside holidays in order to observe the first universal exhibition of the Republic and to give lengthy accounts of it to *Le Messager de l'Europe* of St. Petersburg. Despite his family

138. Paris at night: one of the rare photographs of this type taken by Zola.

139

problems—his daughter, Denise, was born in September—the writer was nonetheless an enthusiastic participant in the 1889 fair. But more than any of the preceding fairs, that of 1900 seems to have filled Zola with excitement: he would spend many hours there and take hundreds of snapshots. Few, indeed, are the pavilions that managed to escape his lens. The author of *Les Rougon-Macquart*, in his fashion, celebrated the dawn of a new century. But just as its contemporaries could not have known that the eighteenth century would end on the plains of Waterloo, one could not predict in 1900 that the nineteenth century would find its veritable end only on August 2, 1914, when the young people on either side of the border would shout: "To Berlin!" and "To Paris!"

139 to 141. Three recently discovered photographs of the World's Fair taken at night by Zola. In those days, few photographers risked taking nighttime photographs, since the sensitivity of the film then available made it unlikely the pictures would turn out successfully.

142. The Pont d'Iéna.   143. A restaurant along the Seine.

144

144. The Pont des Invalides. 145. The main entrance to the World's Fair, known as the Monumental Gate. Placed at a southwest angle from the place de la Concorde, the gate was crowned by a large allegorical statue in the guise of a Parisian dressed in the fashion of the day that personified the city of Paris welcoming her guests. Covered with polychrome decoration and surrounded by 3,200 incandescent lights and 40 arc lamps, the monument consisted of a hemispheric dome resting on three arches between two 115-foot-high minarets of Byzantine and Persian inspiration. 146. The pavilions of the foreign powers: (from left to right) Germany, Spain, Monaco, Sweden, and Greece. The portion of the Pont de l'Alma open to general circulation and, to the left, the footbridge.

145

146

148

147. The Creusot Pavilion of iron and steel metallurgy.   148. The waterworks and the Palace of Electricity. Both a diadem and a fan, the monument was crowned with an allegorical figure by the sculptor Laurent-Honoré Marqueste. Eighteen feet tall and standing naked in a carriage drawn by Pegasus and a dragon, the statue represented the Electricity Fairy.

"Now, I understand the attraction the Machine Arcade had for my father in the Champ de Mars during the Fair of 1900. We spent hours there. Clearly fascinated, my father looked, listened; me, I admit that those masses of iron, those wheels turning with an indescribable racket, did not interest me a bit, while Jacques followed our father step by step and barraged him with questions." (Denise Le Blond-Zola, Émile Zola raconté par sa fille)

149

149 to 151. The mobile platform or "moving sidewalk." Two miles long, the platform was made up of three sections: a fixed sidewalk and two continuously moving sidewalks (the first of which went at a speed of 2.5 miles per hour and the second at 5.5 miles per hour). The passengers got onto the platform on the fixed side, from which they could easily cross over first to the slower moving sidewalk, then to the faster one. To get off the platform, they did the same in reverse. 152. The electric train also made a full circuit around the fair (but in the opposite direction) in twenty minutes and at the cost of half a franc. 153. The Celestial Globe. 154. The Eiffel Tower seen from the gardens of the Trocadéro.

150

151

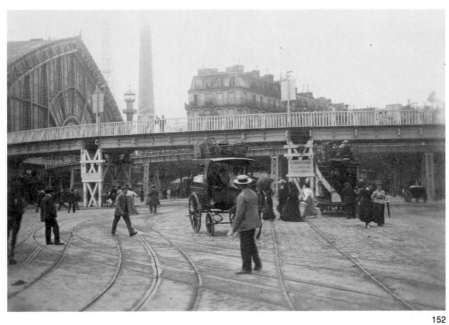

152

155

155. Shot taken from the stairs of the Eiffel Tower. View of the gardens of the Champ de Mars and the Palace of Electricity below.
156. Shot taken from the second floor of the Eiffel Tower. The Trocadéro, built for the 1878 fair and replaced by the Palais de Chaillot in the 1937 fair. To the right of the Trocadéro, the Pavilion of the Russian Empire, and, on either side of the Pont d'Iéna, exotic restaurants.

"Once again, here we are facing this contemporary architecture about which I have spoken and which expresses the style of the nineteenth century with its audacious cast-iron structures that are at once so light and so solid." (Zola, Letter from Paris to the Messager de l'Europe *of St. Petersburg)*

157

157 and 158. Shots of a restaurant and a pavilion taken from above.

159. The Swiss Village, a reconstruction of chalets from the Valais.   160. The Pont d'Iéna.   161. The Great Wheel, which survived the fair (it was demolished in 1910).

159

160

162

162. General view of the fair.

Portraits
and Still Lifes

163

163. Zola with one of the cameras he used
for his portraits.   164 to 183. Different
photographic avatars of Jeanne. Zola's interest in three-quarter shots, rare for the
period, is notable (see especially photographs 178, 179, 182, and 183).   184 to
188. Zola and Jeanne.   189 to 192. Zola.
Note his face without spectacles, rather unusual (189).   193. Zola and his children
around 1902.   194. Denise.   195 to 197.
Jacques.   198 and 199. Denise.   200.
Jacques.   201. Denise and Jacques.

170

171

172

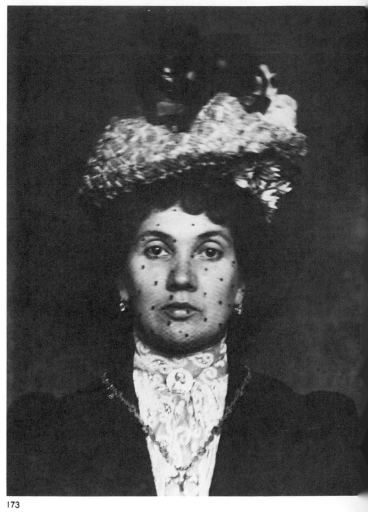

173

154

175

176

178

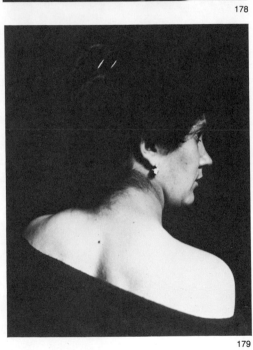

179

180

181

182

159

184

185

161

187

188

163

190

191

193

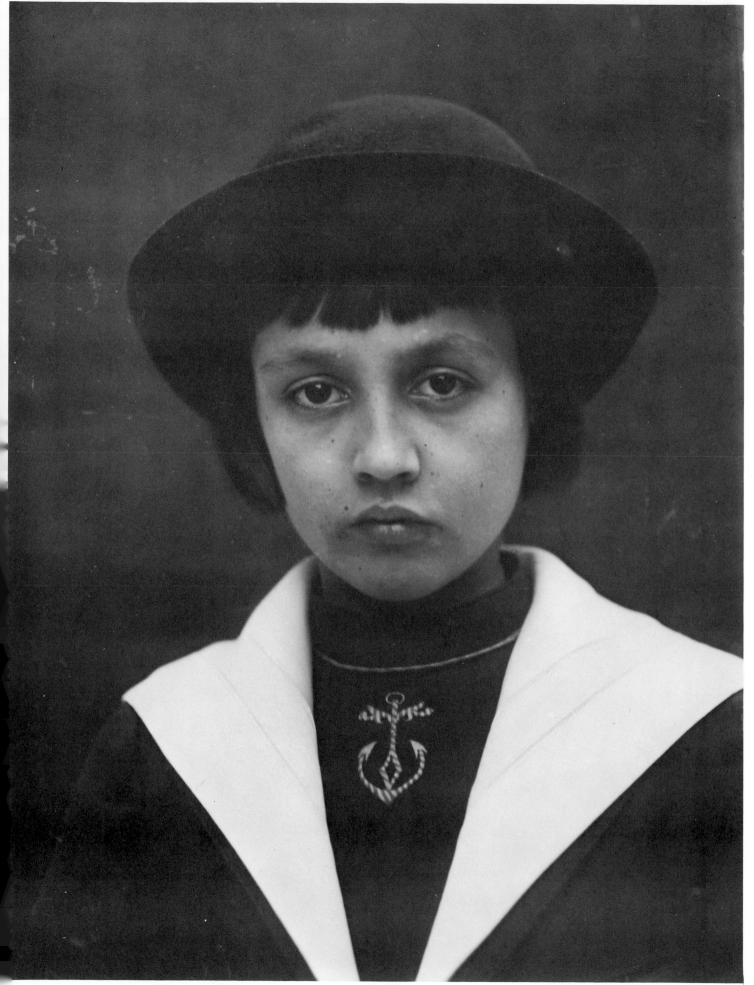

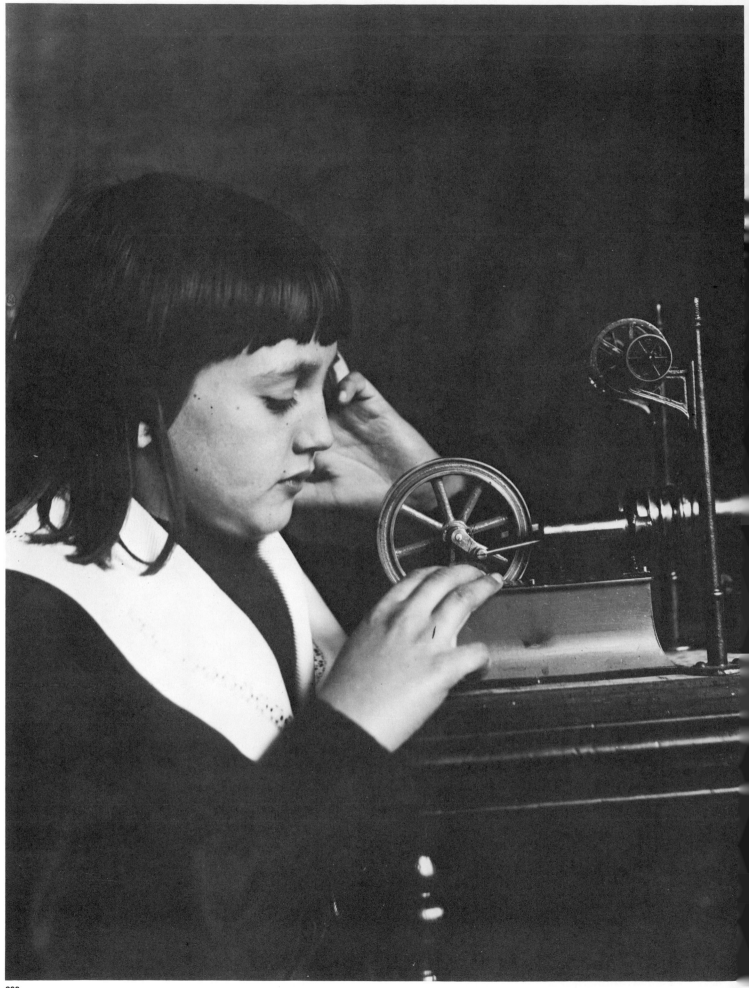

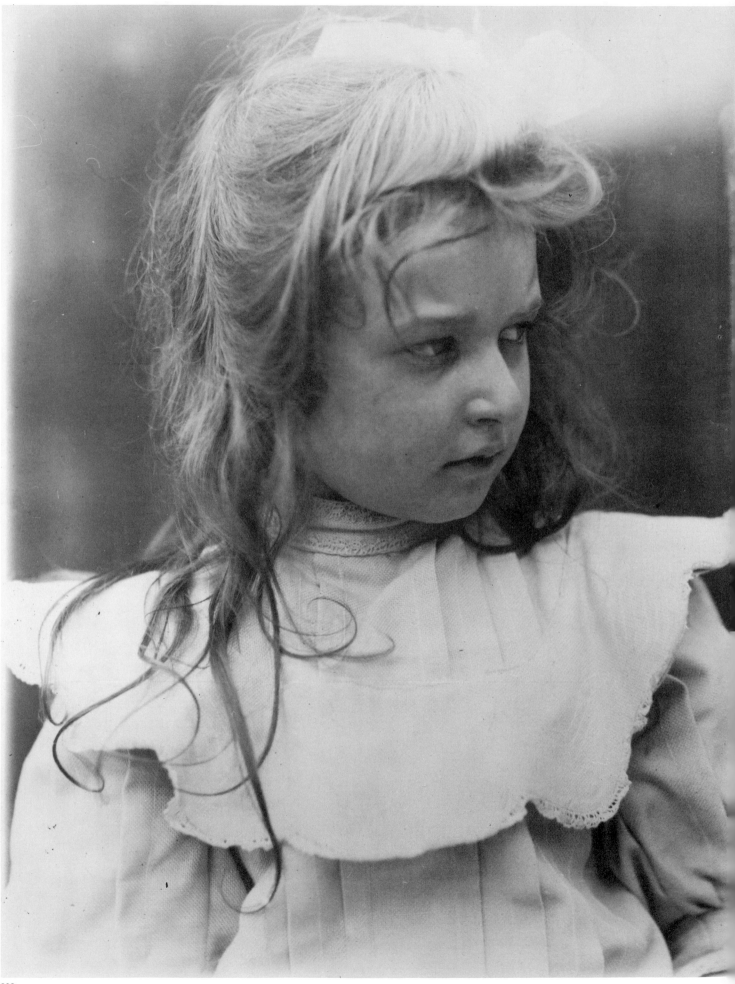

204

205

207

202. Paulette Brulat (daughter of Paul Brulat, a friend of Zola's who published a book on the Dreyfus affair in 1898). 203. Georges Charpentier (1846–1905), Zola's and Alexis's editor. "He had the audacity," wrote Zola, "to gather us together at a time when the doors were still shutting in our faces." (*Les Romanciers naturalistes*) 204. Daguerreotype of Zola, age six, resting on a stack of *Les Rougon-Macquart*, symbol of a life of work, battle, and victory. The Alexandre Charpentier bronze medal dates from January 1899. (A gold copy of it was given to the Bibliothèque nationale.) 205. Manet's portrait of Zola, photographed by the writer in the rue de Bruxelles apartment. 206. The foreign editions of *Les Trois villes* and *Les Quatre Évangiles* framing a daguerreotype of the engineer François Zola with his son. 207. Zola and Alexandrine. 208. The little family hand in hand.

181

208